The Chain & Crystal Book

INTERSTELLAR

TRADING & PUBLISHING COMPANY

LOS ANGELES, CALIFORNIA

ISBN 0-9645957-7-X
LIBRARY OF CONGRESS CATALOG NUMBER: 97-93594
SAN: 298-5829

All illustrations by Wendy Simpson Conner
Color Photography by Don Brandos
Printed in the United States of America

FIRST PRINTING: MARCH, 1997
SECOND PRINTING: JUNE, 2000
THIRD PRINTING: DECEMBER, 2002

310-247-8154
Please visit our website at www.interstellarpublishing.com

ACKNOWLEDGMENTS:
To Jennie, Priscilla, Joni and Paul;
and everyone who bought and loved
THE BEST LITTLE BEADING BOOK,
THE BEADED LAMPSHADE BOOK,
THE MAGICAL BEADED MEDICINE BAG BOOK.
THE 'KNOTTY' MACRAME AND BEADING BOOK
THE BEADED WATCHBAND BOOK
AND ALL OF OUR OTHER BOOKS

Introduction

Crystal is timeless. I don't know anyone who doesn't love crystal. The way it catches the light, the beautiful way it looks when worn: crystal enhances everything. Combining crystal with chain is a great way to have that elegance at a fraction of the price of a solid strung strand. Sometimes crystal does get a bit pricy, so it's nice when you can have the look without the high pricetag. Some of the necklaces in this book use as few as 5 crystal beads. I've also taken artistic license, and included projects that aren't just crystal, but also glass beads, or semiprecious. The intent is to give you lots of latitude with this jewelry: there's a look for everyone.

Try garage sales or antique malls for your crystal - there are some great treasures out there. The old crystal is the best - some of the unusual cuts and shapes just aren't made anymore. If you ask your relatives for old jewelry, you will be amazed at what they have hidden in old cigar boxes and old cookie tins. One lady I know cleaned out her garage and found boxes and boxes of rare old Austrian and Czech crystal from the turn of the century. She had been given the boxes years earlier when her aunt died, and never bothered to open them. She took one necklace to an antique appraiser, and found it was worth $3,600! Some of the old crystal necklaces are worth something as is, so you may want to look them up in a collector's book before you take them apart.

Another thing to look for is bags of broken strands - I got a one-quart size ziplock bag of crystal at the flea market for $5. Some were broken pieces, but at least three quarters of it was vintage crystal: well worth the investment!

This is part of a series of 25 books called **The Beading Books Series.** Other books in the series include *The Best Little Beading Book, The Beaded Lampshade Book, The Magical Beaded Medicine Bag Book, The "Knotty" Macrame and Beading Book* and *The Beaded Watchband Book.*

As always, I love hearing your wonderful comments. Please feel free to write to me c/o The Interstellar Trading and Publishing Company, Post Office Box 2215, La Mesa, CA 91943.

Happy Beading!™

"Me"

Table of Contents

Table of Contents

TYPES OF CHAIN

The right chain can either make or break your design. If using larger beads, you want the chain to "hold its own", yet with more delicate beads, you wouldn't want the chain to overpower them.

There is also the problem of easy-to-maneuver links. Some chains just don't lend themselves to these types of designs because they just don't have links that can open to accommodate wires and eyepins.

The following table should help in choosing a chain design.

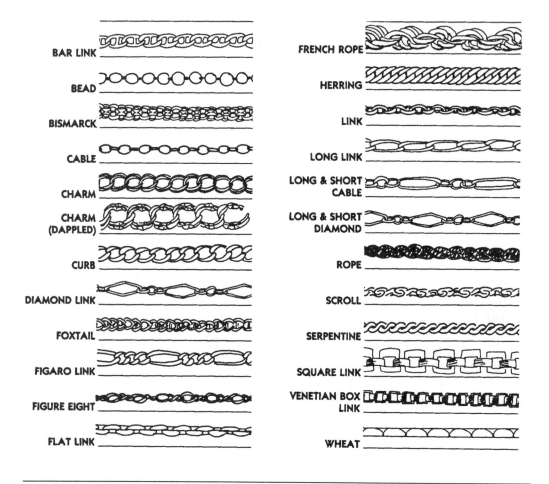

BAR LINK		FRENCH ROPE	
BEAD		HERRING	
BISMARCK		LINK	
CABLE		LONG LINK	
CHARM		LONG & SHORT CABLE	
CHARM (DAPPLED)		LONG & SHORT DIAMOND	
CURB		ROPE	
DIAMOND LINK		SCROLL	
FOXTAIL		SERPENTINE	
FIGARO LINK		SQUARE LINK	
FIGURE EIGHT		VENETIAN BOX LINK	
FLAT LINK		WHEAT	

DIFFERENCES IN WIRE

There are several types of wire available for you to use with your projects. When using real sterling silver, gold or gold-filled chain, you're better off matching it with compatible wire.

Remember that gold is very soft, gold filled is stronger, and sterling is also on the soft side. There may be times when you're better off using an inexpensive (strong) goldtone or silvertone chain, instead of the real thing. You can then work with jeweler's wire (which is plated over copper or other base metals), or other inexpensive variations.

Sterling, gold and gold-filled wires come in hard, half-hard and soft. This refers to the ease of manipulating the wire. Unfortunately, a softer wire will be a dream to work with, but a nightmare when it comes to durability. I like to use half-hard wires, because you get the best of both worlds.

Wires also come in gauges, which refers to the thickness. The higher the number, the thinner the wire, so a 24 will be heavier than a 32. Again, you will have to trade off the ease of working with the wire with the lasting quality of the finished product. Some of the projects in this book require a 22 gauge wire (medium weight, yet durable), some use an 18 weight (can be difficult to work with), and some use 24 (easy to wirewrap your loops). Try experimenting to see what works best for you.

Also, look for wires in unusual colors. Jeweler's wire comes in black, red, green and purple, which adds some variety to your work. The hardest thing might be finding chain to match, although there are ways to color your chain (please see page 11).

CRYSTAL & OTHER BEADS

There are different types of crystal. **Austrian crystal**, known for its brilliant fire, has a high lead content that gives the crisp, accurate cut of the facets.

Czech firepolished crystal has a softer look (due to the lower lead content), but still retains the brilliance in colors. It is less brittle than the Austrian, doesn't shatter as easily, and tends to be more durable. Personally, I prefer working with Czech crystal, because it is reasonably priced and looks so nice.

There are also **plastic beads that resemble crystal**, but unless you are making this for a child, it's not really worth your putting so much work into a piece when the materials are degrading to the finished design. You're better off using real crystal.

Crystal comes in several shapes.

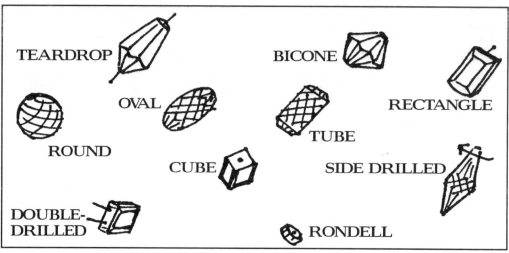

They also come in many colors and sizes. There is quite a variety to choose from. Even think about using old chandelier crystals.

As for other beads, you can adapt any of the designs in this book to what you have available in your bead box. Half the fun is experimenting!

CHARMS AND CONNECTORS

There are many ways to link sections of chain to other sections of chain and beads.

The easiest way is to use a jumpring. This is a circle of wire that holds its shape. Be careful when you open the jumpring that you swivel it sideways, not pull it back, which \will distort the curve. Always make sure you've closed it completely. If using sterling or gold, you may want to solder the jumpring shut.

A split ring is like a little key ring. It's trickier to use, but you won't run the risk of it opening.

Use eye pins as a link to hold your beads and connect to chain.

Double ended charms and findings of all kinds can be used.

Also, the latest thing are the Bali silver connectors with semi-precious stones in them (you'll find them at gemshows). You can coordinate these in garnet, pearl, citrine, amethyst, and more. There are matching pendants.

PLIERS AND TOOLS

As in any art, the tools you use have a lot to do with the success of your piece. Just as a painter must use the right brush, so must you have the right pliers. Many people don't realize how using the wrong tools can undermine their efforts, and make the job harder.

You will ruin your tweezers if you try to use them to manipulate metal. They are just not made to be worked with that way. You will be much happier if you own a selection of pliers - it makes it a lot easier to be able to grip with two at a time.

The pliers shown below are the best for the job at hand.

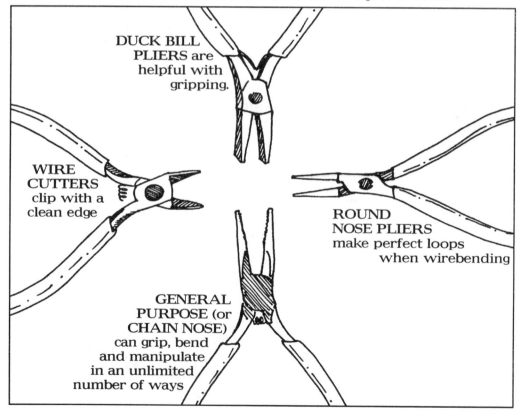

DUCK BILL PLIERS are helpful with gripping.

WIRE CUTTERS clip with a clean edge

ROUND NOSE PLIERS make perfect loops when wirebending

GENERAL PURPOSE (or CHAIN NOSE) can grip, bend and manipulate in an unlimited number of ways

ENHANCING YOUR DESIGNS

Beyond the use of brightly colored crystals and beads, there are other ways of getting color into your jewelry.

Patinas are ways to change the color of the metal itself (usually done with sterling or gold) to produce an antiqued effect. There are many patinas on the market today, and you can change your chain to antiqued black, blue, green, or deep antiqued gold and silver. The trick to the patina staying with the metal and not rubbing off and fading has a lot to do with how you prepare the metal's surface before you start. Oils from your skin will cause contamination, and the patina will not "bite" properly. You need to clean the surface just before you patina it.

You can use muriatic acid (for heaven's sake, read ALL the instructions before you buy this stuff - it's pretty scary). This is what you use in a pool. It burns off all inpurities on the surface of what you want to patina. Use plastic gloves with this, and be careful when you work with it! If you have any questions about muriatic acid, ask the salesclerk at the store where you buy it.

OR, you can burn off impurities with hydrogen peroxide.

When working with the items mentioned above, you want to work quickly and cleanly. This is not for kids! If you have pearls on your jewelry, don't keep them submerged for too long - usually, just a quick dip is all you need. Bend a paperclip to make a utensil for dipping, to keep your hands out of it.

Once you've cleaned off the surface of the chain, you can dip in the patina. The longer you leave it, the darker it will be. Again, watch out for those pearls! Rinse and dry on a papertowel when done.

Of course, you can always take the easy way out and buy chain and wire that's already been colored.

You can also buy special markers made for coloring metal - use them on charms, chain, etc. You can even use the touch-up paint from your car for this!

COLOR PHOTO INDEX

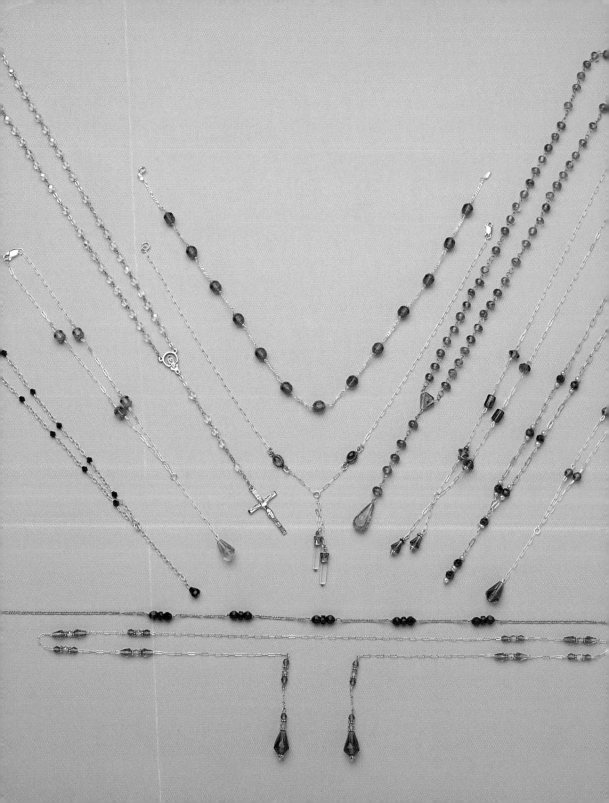

SIMPLE WIRELOOPING

The easiest and quickest method for linking chain to beads is to use wire or eye pins, and wirebend the ends into the end link of chain to make a continuous length with a design.

To make simple loops:

STEP ONE:

Thread your beads on the eye pin or wire in the desired design.

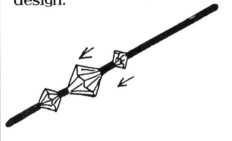

STEP TWO:

With the round nose plier, make a loop in the wire on one side. Try to use a smooth rolling motion. Roll the wire over the end of the plier. The size of the loop will depend on how much wire is in your loop (generally, 1/2" per loop is plenty), and how close you are to the tip of the plier.

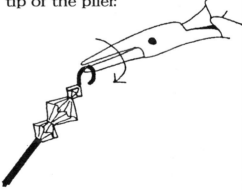

Be sure that your loop is completely closed.

STEP THREE:

Repeat on the second side. Work snugly, so there's not a lot of "wiggle" between beads. Trim off any excess wire ends.

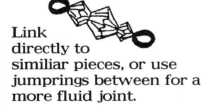

Link directly to similiar pieces, or use jumprings between for a more fluid joint.

WRAPPED LOOPS

This takes a little more practice, and there is a great variety of results. Try different gauges of wire for special effects.

To make wirewrapped loops:

STEP ONE:

Work directly from the spool of wire. Thread your beads onto the wire (bend it back with about 3" lead end).

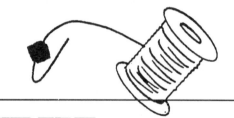

STEP THREE:

Repeat for the second side.

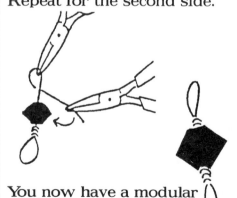

You now have a modular component.

STEP TWO:

Hold your wire with one plier, and grab the wire end with the other.

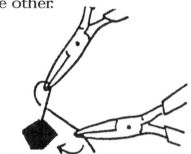

Twist the end around the wire shaft in a smooth motion. Work tightly.

Trim off any excess wire from your looped end.

DESIGN IDEAS

Now that you've worked with some of the technique, now it's time to start thinking about composition. There are literally thousands (maybe even millions) of designs out there in the universe, but certain ones seem to always be popular. On this and the next page, there are just a few of the possibilities.

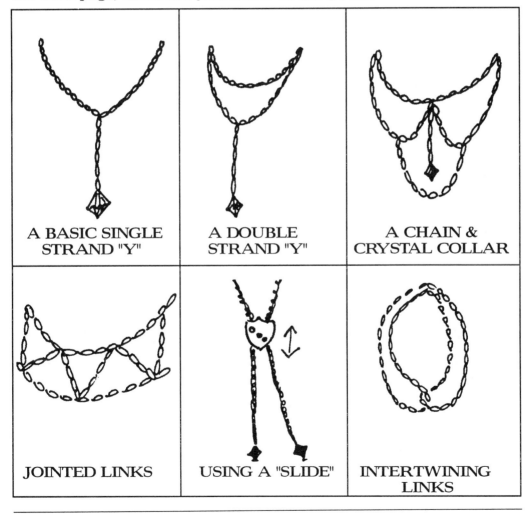

A BASIC SINGLE STRAND "Y"	A DOUBLE STRAND "Y"	A CHAIN & CRYSTAL COLLAR
JOINTED LINKS	USING A "SLIDE"	INTERTWINING LINKS

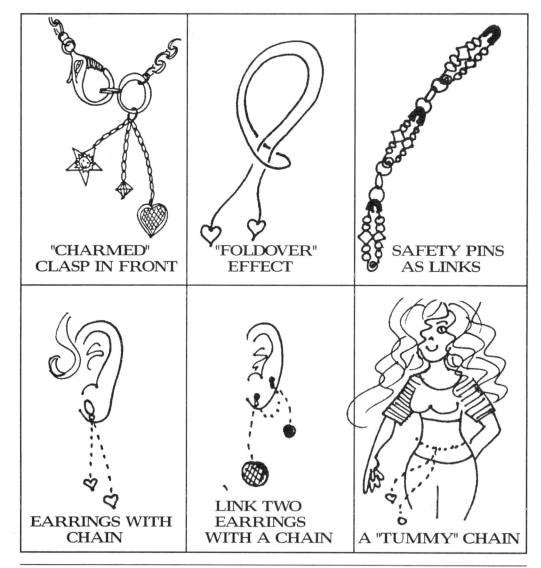

"CHARMED"
CLASP IN FRONT

"FOLDOVER"
EFFECT

SAFETY PINS
AS LINKS

EARRINGS WITH
CHAIN

LINK TWO
EARRINGS
WITH A CHAIN

A "TUMMY" CHAIN

INDIAN GLASS BEAD CHOKER

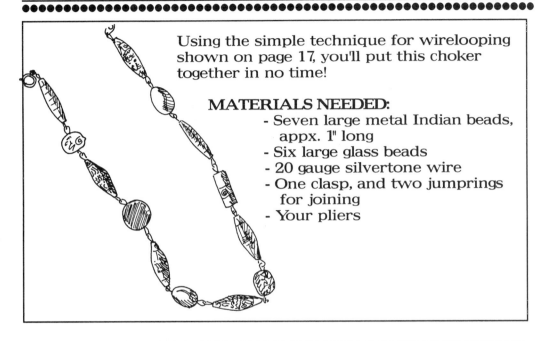

Using the simple technique for wirelooping shown on page 17, you'll put this choker together in no time!

MATERIALS NEEDED:
- Seven large metal Indian beads, appx. 1" long
- Six large glass beads
- 20 gauge silvertone wire
- One clasp, and two jumprings for joining
- Your pliers

CRYSTAL DOVE NECKLACE

Use the same technique on this necklace, but use little bird charms as links.

MATERIALS NEEDED:
- Ten to twelve double linked bird charms (number depends on size - these were 5/8" long)
- Appx. 15 7x5mm crystal beads (use more in back near the clasp so it lays smoothly)
- 24 gauge silvertone wire
- One clasp, and two jumprings for joining
- Your pliers

BLACK & GOLD GLASS NECKLACE

This necklace looks very elegant for evening, work, or anytime. Black is the "instant dressup color" - and the combination with gold is very nice. Texture plays a big part in this necklace - look for coordinating beads with rich textures and designs. Make this one longer, so you can wear it with turtleneck sweaters. You can even make it long enough to go over your head without a clasp!

Use the wrapped loop technique shown on page 18 . . . it really adds to the richness.

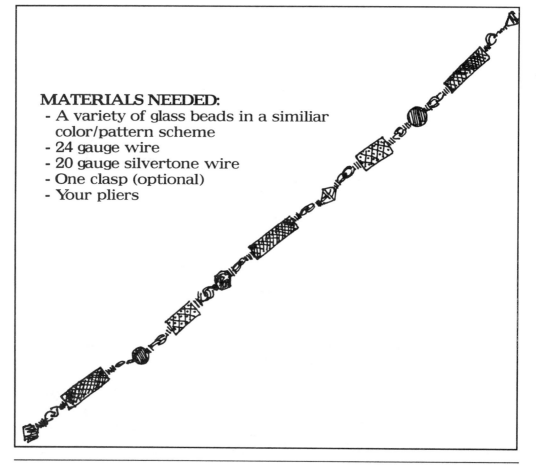

MATERIALS NEEDED:
- A variety of glass beads in a similiar color/pattern scheme
- 24 gauge wire
- 20 gauge silvertone wire
- One clasp (optional)
- Your pliers

FLUORITE & GLASS NECKLACE

The thing that really catches your eye with this necklace is the lavender wire. It's subtle, yet looks so great. You can make this long enough to not need a clasp.

MATERIALS NEEDED:
- Fifteen one-inch-long glass beads
- Thirteen 4mm irridescent fucshia glass beads
- 22 gauge lavender wire
- One 40mm fluorite pi bead
- Your pliers

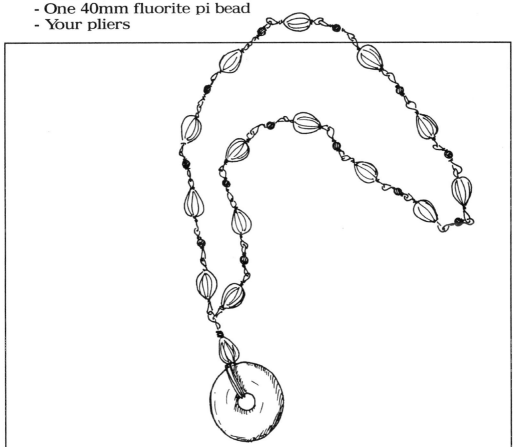

FLUORITE & GLASS NECKLACE

STEP ONE:

Wrap the pi bead with lavender wire as shown.

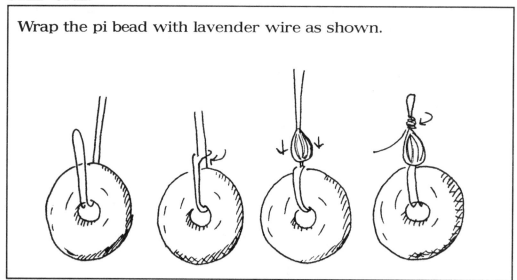

STEP TWO:

Link the beads as shown.

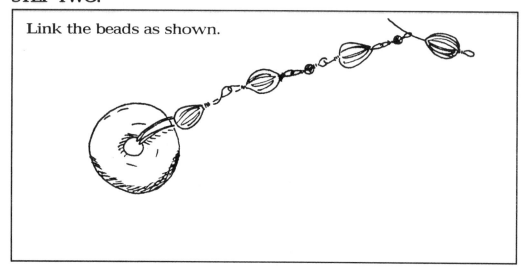

ENHANCED CHAIN & LOCKET NECKLACE

Even if you don't want to do an entire necklace mixing beads and chain, you can still jazz up a store bought chain by adding a few beads. Sterling and garnet are one of my favorite combinations, and these beads add so much to the look!

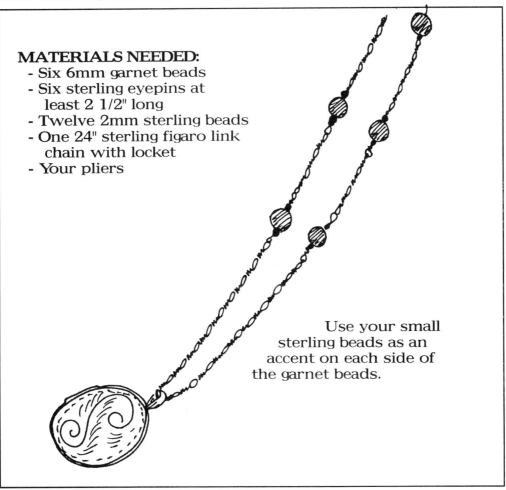

MATERIALS NEEDED:
- Six 6mm garnet beads
- Six sterling eyepins at least 2 1/2" long
- Twelve 2mm sterling beads
- One 24" sterling figaro link chain with locket
- Your pliers

Use your small sterling beads as an accent on each side of the garnet beads.

THREE EASY PIECES

Now that you're a pro at this linking thing, you can practically do it in your sleep! Take your projects with you - these work up quickly, and many times people see you working on them and want to buy them on the spot! These 3 necklaces are just the beginning!

CHERRY AMBER & SILVER NECKLACE:

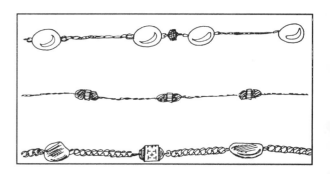

MATERIALS NEEDED:
- Twenty large cherry amber beads
- Twenty eye pins, or a length of 22 gauge wire
- Ten silver double sided connectors
- 12 - 14" of "French rope" chain
- Your pliers

COBALT BLUE CRYSTAL:

MATERIALS NEEDED:
- Ten 6mm cobalt Czech crystals
- Five cobalt rondell crystals
- Ten eye pins, or a length of 22 gauge wire
- One 16" figaro link sterling chain necklace
- Your pliers
OPTIONAL: patina

AMETHYST & STERLING:

MATERIALS NEEDED:
- Four large drilled amethyst nuggets
- Three sterling beads
- Seven eye pins or #22 wire
- One 16" "double charm" link chain.
- your pliers

If you work with a ready-made chain necklace, you don't have to worry about adding or soldering a clasp. Just measure from your centerpoint and add beads as needed! Don't worry if your chain is too short - you can always add more beads to lengthen it.

MAKING A ROSARY

Handmade Rosaries make a wonderful gift. You can make rosaries out of crystal, birthstones, beads that have been in the family for years . . . almost any type of bead will do.

MATERIALS NEEDED:
- Fifty beads of one type (main bead)
- Nine beads that are similiar or different (spacer beads)
- #20 or #22 gauge wire
- One crucifix
- One Rosary centerpiece
- Sixteen jumprings
- Your pliers

You can link your Rosary with simple loops. The pattern is 10 main beads, one jump ring, one spacer bead, one jump ring, 10 main beads, one jump ring, one spacer bead, one jump ring, 10 main beads, one jump ring, one spacer bead, one jump ring, 10 main beads, one jump ring, one spacer bead, one jump ring, 10 main beads. Be sure that it begins and ends with the 10 main beads.

Connect each end to the two side loops of the centerpiece, using 2 jump rings per side.

"Y" NECKLACES

Unless you've been on Mars for the last few years, you can't help but notice these cute little "minimalist" necklaces. Mainly chain, they use a minimum of (usually) crystal beads. It's a design that dates back to Victorian times. It's very elegant, and looks great with either an evening gown or a blazer. There are literally thousands of variations, here are but a few.

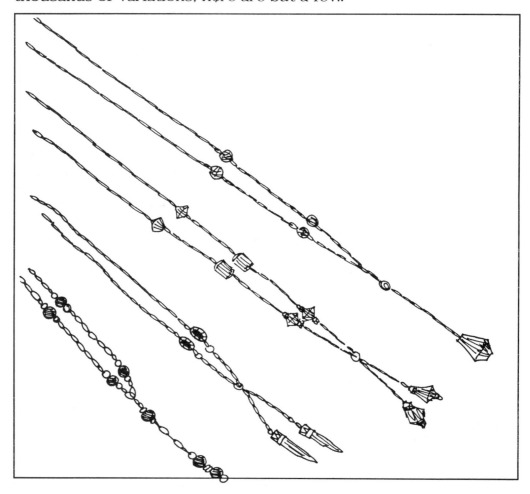

"Y" NECKLACES - 4 VARIATIONS

●●

These necklaces all use the same basic technique, the main differences are in materials.

GOLD FILLED/PEARL AND GARNET NECKLACE:
MATERIALS NEEDED:
- One 20" goldfilled long link chain with clasp
- Nine 5mm faceted garnet beads
- Eighteen champaign-colored fresh water pearls
- Eight gold filled eye pins (or wire) and one head pin*
   (*the gauge is determined by the size of the holes in the pearls)

TERMINATED CRYSTAL & STERLING NECKLACE:
I actually took apart a pair of earrings to make this necklace.
MATERIALS NEEDED:
- One 20" sterling long link chain with clasp
- Two terminated crystals with fancy silver caps
- Two amethyst and silver earring connectors
- Seven jumprings

MONTANA SAPPHIRE & SILVER NECKLACE:
MATERIALS NEEDED;
- One 20" sterling long link chain with clasp
- Four 6mm Montana sapphire crystals, bicone shaped
- Two 8x6mm Montana sapphire crystals, rectangle shaped
- Two 6mm Montana sapphire crystals, teardrop shaped
- Six Bali silver bead caps (4mm)
- A length of 22 gauge wire, plus 2 fancy head pins that match the design in the Bali silver beadcaps (the heads of the headpin are ornate)

BASIC "Y" NECKLACE:
MATERIALS NEEDED:
- One 20" sterling long link chain with clasp
- Five 5mm round beads, plus 1 14mm teardrop shape bead
- length of 22 gauge wire, plus one head pin
- One jumpring

LANIERE DESIGNS

This is basically a "y" necklace on steroids. It's longer, has more beads, and is made to be worn over a sweater, where the "y" necklace is usually worn shorter at the bare throat. This can incorporate an old Rosary, or even just odds and ends of beads.

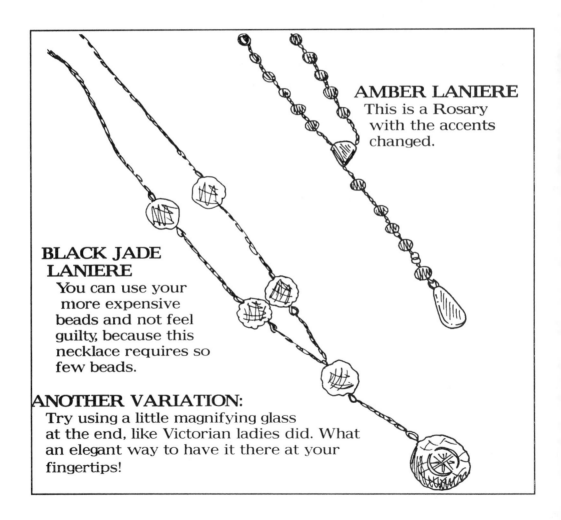

AMBER LANIERE
This is a Rosary with the accents changed.

BLACK JADE LANIERE
You can use your more expensive beads and not feel guilty, because this necklace requires so few beads.

ANOTHER VARIATION:
Try using a little magnifying glass at the end, like Victorian ladies did. What an elegant way to have it there at your fingertips!

EASY LARIAT

This is probably one of the most versatile designs there is. You can wear it just hung over your shoulders, or tied loosely in an overhand knot in front, around your waist as a "tummy cord" . . . there's lots of variations.

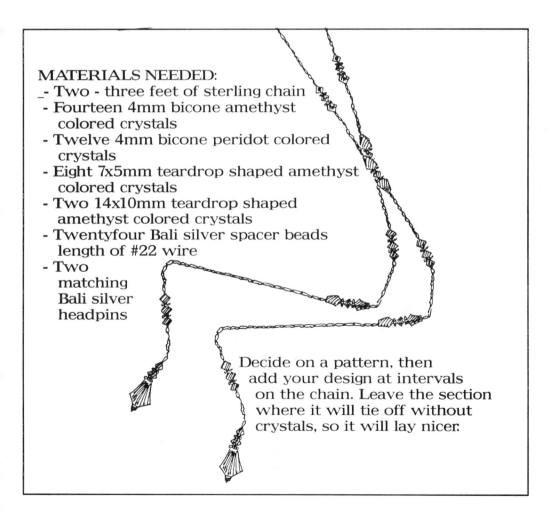

MATERIALS NEEDED:
- Two - three feet of sterling chain
- Fourteen 4mm bicone amethyst colored crystals
- Twelve 4mm bicone peridot colored crystals
- Eight 7x5mm teardrop shaped amethyst colored crystals
- Two 14x10mm teardrop shaped amethyst colored crystals
- Twentyfour Bali silver spacer beads length of #22 wire
- Two matching Bali silver headpins

Decide on a pattern, then add your design at intervals on the chain. Leave the section where it will tie off without crystals, so it will lay nicer.

BEES & BUTTERFLIES NECKLACE

You will find this to be extremely easy to put together, and you will always get comments everytime you wear it. It costs almost nothing to make, yet people really like it.

MATERIALS NEEDED:
- Fifteen bezeled 3mm red crystal double-sided connectors
- One 5mm bezeled red crystal single-sided connector
- Eight bee charms
- Six butterfly charms
- One larger sunflower charm
- Thirty one 4mm jumprings
- One delicate goldfilled chain

BEES & BUTTERFLIES NECKLACE

DIRECTIONS:

Use your jumprings to connect your components, making sure that they all face the same way. Start with the centerpiece, then build out at even intervals, alternating your charms.

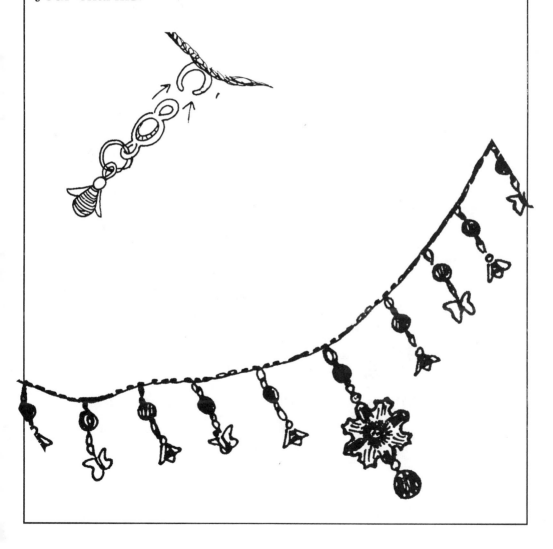

PEWTERTONE & BLACK

Pewter is a very popular metal color this year - it really stands out from the softer, lighter metal shades. Teamed with black, it really comes alive!

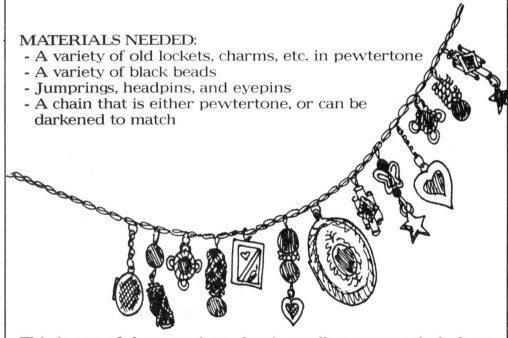

MATERIALS NEEDED:
- A variety of old lockets, charms, etc. in pewtertone
- A variety of black beads
- Jumprings, headpins, and eyepins
- A chain that is either pewtertone, or can be darkened to match

This is one of those projects that is totally asymmetrical - have fun with using anything you find that you like the look of. You're matching colors more than shape, so this gives you a lot of freedom with the design process.

NOAH'S ARK NECKLACE

Making a theme necklace like this is a lot of fun. It stimulates great imagination, and you end up with something really fun to wear.

MATERIALS NEEDED:
- A length of chain with a clasp
- An assortment of themed charms (animals, Noah's ark, etc.)
- Thirteen 5mm green firepolished irridescent crystals
- Jumprings and headpins

Add your
    animals at
        intervals.
            Use your
                crystal beads
                    as accents.

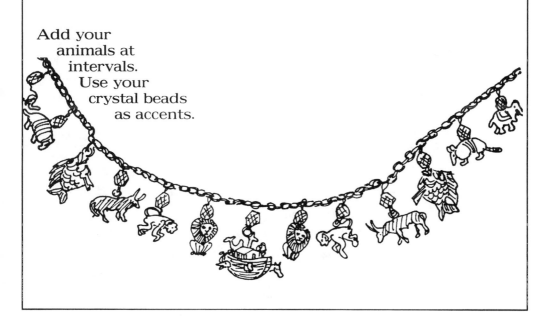

GYPSY TRINKET CHARM NECKLACE #1

Now it all gets to be REALLY fun! You can go to town with this one - old gum machine toys, earring parts, ANYTHING GOES! Even try the metal paints on your findings for lots of color.

MATERIALS NEEDED:
- A length of chain with a clasp
- An assortment of odds and ends: charms, beads, little toys, etc.
- Jumprings and headpins

This is a variation of the previous necklace, yet each one looks so different!

MATERIALS NEEDED:
- A length of chain with a clasp
- An assortment of odds and ends: charms, beads, little toys, etc.
- Jumprings and headpins

If you're using side-drilled crystal (many of the old antique crystal is drilled this way), then you will need to make your own "bails" to attach the crystal.

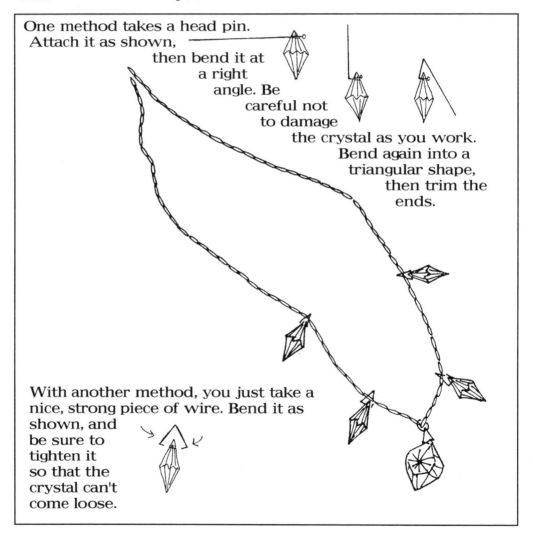

One method takes a head pin. Attach it as shown, then bend it at a right angle. Be careful not to damage the crystal as you work. Bend again into a triangular shape, then trim the ends.

With another method, you just take a nice, strong piece of wire. Bend it as shown, and be sure to tighten it so that the crystal can't come loose.

You can buy these components so cheaply at gemshows, and make a spectacular necklace that looks like an antique!

MATERIALS NEEDED:
- A length of chain
  with a clasp
- Connectors
- Jumprings

RHINESTONE & CHAIN

This necklace is actually composed of several parts from earrings.It is perfectly ok to buy inexpensive jewelry and use the pieces. The rhinestones are so elegant, and sometimes it is impossible to find findings in their loose state that will do the job.

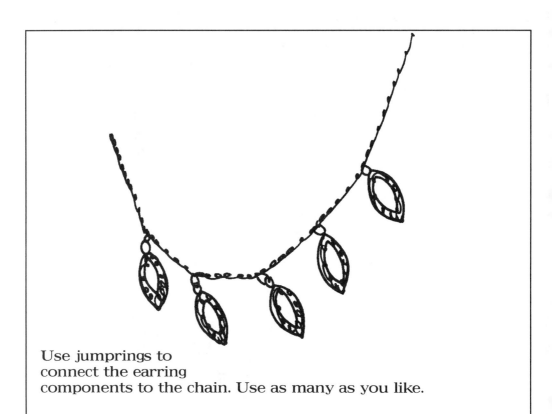

Use jumprings to connect the earring components to the chain. Use as many as you like.

Taking the previous concepts one step further, you can interlock many components into an almost "chainmail" type effect.

MATERIALS NEEDED:
- Five lapis single-sided connectors
- Five lapis double-sided connectors
- Fourteen jumprings
- Length of chain with a clasp

Use your jumprings
to link these
components
together.
Be as
crazy
with it
as
you
like!

There is no end to the ideas with this technique!

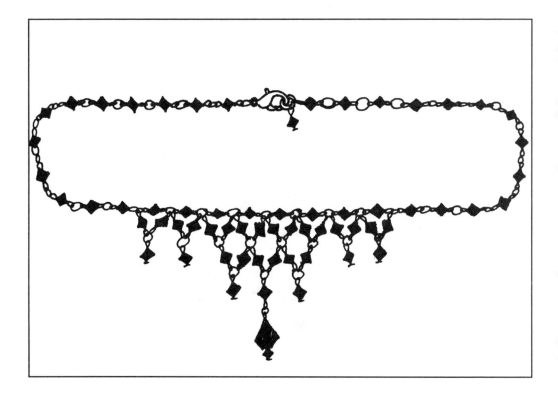

INTERLOCKING COLLAR

MATERIALS NEEDED:
- Sixty-one 4mm bicone shaped jet crystal beads
- One 10mm bicone shaped jet crystal bead
- One clasp
- Jumprings
- 22 gauge wire
- Eight head pins

DIRECTIONS:

Start by putting fifty-three 4mm crystal on a length of wire with a loop at both ends.

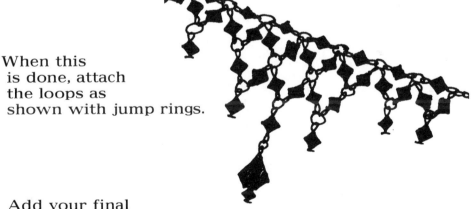

When this is done, attach the loops as shown with jump rings.

Add your final beads on headpins as shown.

BLUE CRYSTAL INTERLOCKING COLLAR

You can really have a good time with this technique! This is easy and very elegant. The sapphire lustre crystal adds so much!

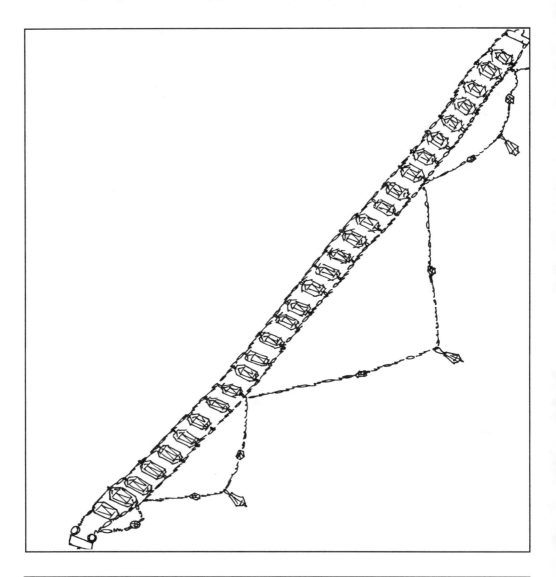

CRYSTAL INTERLOCKING COLLAR

MATERIALS NEEDED:
- Twenty-nine 10x7mm Czech rectangular crystals in sapphire blue lustre
- Six 4mm bicone of matching crystal
- Three 7x5mm triangular matching crystal
- Appx. a yard of chain
- Two necklace bars
- One clasp
- Six jumprings
- 22 gauge wire

STEP ONE:

Put your rectangular crystal on your wire, with loops on each side. Use all 29 beads in this manner.

STEP TWO:

Cut a 16" length of chain, and starting from the center, start attaching these beads as shown.

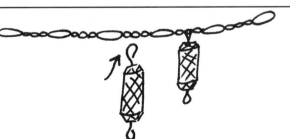

CRYSTAL INTERLOCKING COLLAR

STEP THREE:

Repeat for the other loop on
the other end of each bead.

STEP FOUR:

Working out from the center, link crystal and beads to
add the bottom design.

Finish by using jumprings to connect
your necklace bars and clasp.

CRAZY CONNECTOR NECKLACE

If you sit with a piece of paper and a pencil, the ideas will really start flowing! Have fun with coming up with your own designs for interlocking pieces!

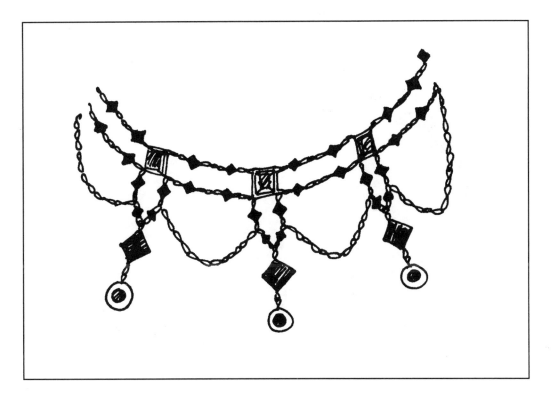

Use **SOFT FLEX™** wire to weave beads in and out of chain.

Use crimp beads to attach
the end, then weave in and
out, adding beads as you
go. End by securing with
crimps.

You can use any of the previous techniques for earrings, too.

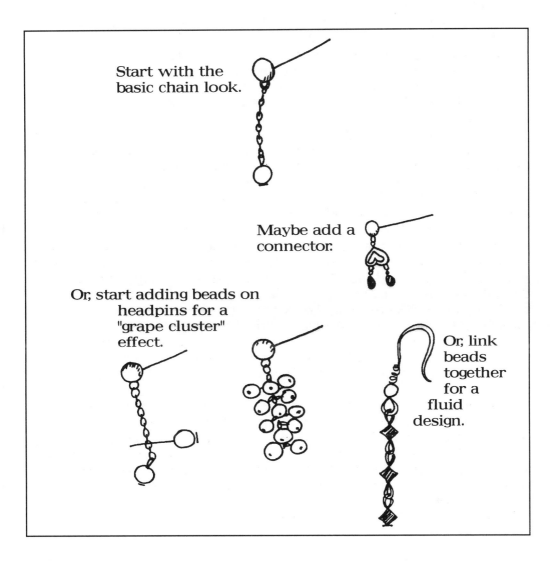

Start with the basic chain look.

Maybe add a connector.

Or, start adding beads on headpins for a "grape cluster" effect.

Or, link beads together for a fluid design.

THE CARE & FEEDING OF CHAIN

Now that you've made all of this wonderful jewelry, how do you keep it looking nice?

There are several things to keep in mind about metals, even before you've made your jewelry.

First of all, real precious metals (gold, gold-filled, and sterling) are more stable than most plated metals (that's part of why it costs more). You may have a tarnishing problem down the road, but this is quickly fixed with a variety of silver-type cleaners on the market.

Or, you can use this handy trick that my friend Elaine suggested: line your sink with tin foil. Put the plug in, so it holds water, and no precious objects can go down the drain (I would still put smaller items in a little plastic bowl just to be sure). Next, fill the sink with about 3-4" of water. Add 2-4 tablespoons of baking soda. Now, add your silver jewelry. There is a chemical reaction that makes the tarnish cling to the tin, not the silver. This is supposed to be a super-easy way to clean your jewelry. Within 5 minutes, your chains should be shiny again. Keep in mind this might wreck your patina. I would also be careful if you have pearls or other delicate beads.

With plated, less expensive chain, you need to be careful of metal's natural enemies: hairspray, perfume, and rubber bands! The hairspray and perfume have alcohol and other chemicals that can break up the plate; for some reason, when rubber bands come into contact with certain metal plating, it turns the metal black.

Also, as you work with chain, if you have been less than careful about how you have packed it up, it will always tangle. With your finer chains, you will end up spending *lightyears* trying to get the tangle out: it's so frustrating! Try to keep some kind of system for wrapping the chain in transporting it - especially if you are carrying several pieces at a time. If you plan ahead, you should have no problem.

Working with chain is a lot of fun. There's really no limit to what you can do!

About the Author

Wendy Simpson Conner is no stranger to beads. As a third-generation bead artist, she grew up with beads from a very early age. Her grandmother was the jewelry and costume designer for the Ziegfeld Follies.

Being from a creative family, Wendy spent her childhood doing many types of crafts in a rural community. ("There just wasn 't anything else to do!"). Over the years, she has mastered many techniques, but beads remained her first love.

She worked as a designer in television for awhile, and also has a strong illustration background (she always insists on doing her own illustrations).

Wendy has been teaching a vocational beadwork class for San Diego Community Colleges and the Grossmont Adult School District for almost fifteen years. She not only teaches beading technique, but also the dynamics of running your own jewelry business.

Wendy designs jewelry for several television shows, as well as the celebrities on them.

She is currently involved with a documentary being made about beads.

Her first book, *The Best Little Beading Book*, was the result of many of her classroom handouts. All of her books, including *The Beaded Lampshade Book*, *The Magical Beaded Medicine Bag Book*, *The "Knotty" Macrame and Beading Book*, and *The Beaded Watchband Book*, have been very popular. They are part of **The Beading Books Series,** a collection of 25 books devoted to preserving beading techniques and history.

Wendy is available to teach workshops. If you are interested, please contact her through the Interstellar Publishing Company, Post Office Box 2215, La Mesa, California, 91943.

INTERSTELLAR

TRADING & PUBLISHING COMPANY

Other Books By the Interstellar Trading & Publishing
Company:

● *The Best Little Beading Book* ●

● *The Beaded Lampshade Book* ●

● *The Magical Beaded Medicine Bag Book* ●

● *The "Knotty" Macrame & Beading Book* ●

● *The Beaded Watchband Book* ●

● *The Beaded Jewelry for a Wedding Book* ●

● *The Crystal and Chain Book* ●

If you would like a list of other titles and forthcoming
books from the Interstellar Trading & Publishing Company,
please send a stamped, self-addressed envelope to:

**THE INTERSTELLAR TRADING & PUBLISHING
COMPANY
POST OFFICE BOX 2215
LA MESA, CALIFORNIA, 91943**